Pure Spirit

SPIRITWRITERSPEAKS

WENDY SHEFFIELD

The right of Wendy Sheffield to be identified as the author of this work has been asserted in accordance with Section 78 of the Copyright, Designs and Patents Act 1988.

Book cover © Wendy Sheffield
Cover image © Proxyminder

This book is published by Compass-Publishing UK.

A CIP record for this book is available from the British Library.

Book ISBN 978-1-912009-39-8

For Sutton Coldfield Spiritualist Church

Contents

Epigraph

[16] *He that heareth you heareth me; and he that despiseth you despiseth me; and he that despiseth me despiseth him that sent me.*
[17] *And the seventy returned again with joy, saying, Lord, even the devils are subject unto us through thy name.*
[18] *And he said unto them, I beheld Satan as lightning fall from heaven.*
[19] *Behold, I give unto you power to tread on serpents and scorpions, and over all the power of the enemy: and nothing shall by any means hurt you.*
(Luke 10:16–19, King James Version)

The Pure Spirit is inside of us. It is waiting patiently to be discovered. It is the pure joy, the unconditional love, the energy that moves everything, the light of God. The Pure Spirit is inside of all of us. It can be awakened. Also, it can be listened to, but not with our ears. Because it requests a spiritual stillness.
(Spiritual Experience, 2022)

Preface

I used to feel alone before I was aware of spirit. (In spiritualism, we use the word 'spirit' to mean the all-encompassing concept of this, as opposed to referring to individual spirits). Now, I'm never alone as I've learnt how to understand and trust my spiritual guidance, which consists of my spirit guide Barnabas, who's a monk (a scribe), and my grandmother, Florence Marjorie Canning.

In this, my second book, I hope to help you feel the love and power of spirit from reading the words within, so as to help you realise you're never alone and there's always someone there for you – you just need to learn how to communicate with your spirit guides, which is easier than you think and certainly nothing to fear! It doesn't matter if you don't know who your spirit guides are; you just need to believe and trust in things that you can't see.

A person's life may consist of travelling many roads before they find their true pathway. Some people sadly never find their true pathway. I was close to remaining on the wrong path for the remainder of my life until my grandmother entered my life in the form of a dream 12 years ago. So, you see, dreams can come true!

My advice to you is not to be afraid and to try different pathways, as this is part of the fabric of life itself. Fortune favours the brave! I know for sure that if I hadn't been brave enough to fight for what I believed in, I wouldn't even have started my new spiritual journey, which has turned my dreams into reality!

Anyone who has read my first book, *Spirit Writer*, will know it's about my spiritual journey and how I came to discover my spiritual gifts and understand my own spiritual journey so I can help others with theirs. Now I've come to terms with my past, my real journey has begun, and I'll now work towards fulfilling my destiny. This isn't about me any more, it's about my sharing my ability as a medium to help others discover their true destiny.

If you want to be able to hear spirit to enable you to receive guidance in your life, or if you just enjoy reading inspirational passages, then this book is for you! My aim is to help you connect better with your inner self, your spirit guides and other people. Once connected, you'll be in a more positive frame of mind, which will enable you to work towards a better life for yourself.

If you've read my first book, you'll be aware that I receive spiritual messages within my mind, and they flow out through my fingers and are typed on a keyboard, which is why spirit refers to me as a 'spirit writer'. (In this book, all such messages are shown in *italics*.)

Spirit is continually working to help people accept that there's an afterlife and no death, just a transition in form. It also wants to help humanity with its understanding of life's trials and tribulations. Of those in your own life, some of them might have been intended to be part of your pathway and others might have been your own doing and shouldn't have happened, so you need to understand which is which. I didn't discover my own pathway until I was in my fifties, just because I listened to other people too much and didn't listen to my inner voice – my inner spirit. Remember, it's up to us whether we want to listen to our messages. We all have free will in the end!

Spirit has a language all of its own, and it isn't easy to put this language into words, as you need to understand not only the messages in your head (which are transmitted telepathically by spirit) but also the messages felt around your body. I'll try to put what I sense into words as best as I can within my messages in this book. All of us have a spiritual sensitivity, and by understanding this, you'll start to trust in your own inner messages, whereupon you'll find that you'll have a better understanding of your life path.

I'll now try to help you visualise what it's like communicating with spirit, so you can recognise the same. Imagine you're walking through a park and you hear the rustling of the trees and the babbling of a brook – this is how spirit communicates, like a child whispering in your ear. On the earth, we listen to sounds that the world makes around us, and over our lifetime, we've learnt how to interpret those sounds. Our interpretation is based on whatever influences have surrounded us throughout our lives. The problem is that different people have learnt during their lives to interpret words in diverse ways to ours and each other's, and therein lies the problem. The background you've been raised within will have a bearing on your interpretation of different words and sounds, which in turn causes misunderstanding between mankind. Spirit believes there will be a time when we'll all accept the same meaning of words, no matter what country you were born in and whatever life you've led; it believes everyone will interpret the words in the same way. One spirit message in this book that relays this message eloquently is called 'Loneliness'. It talks about how, at present, we have all developed our own interpretation of words, but there will come a time when we all will connect better with each other and be as one! Read 'Loneliness' (see page 15) and you'll understand.

Spirit communication is so subtle; at first, you think you're imagining it, but then, as time progresses, you realise that you are starting to know things that you shouldn't know. You then begin to realise that your knowledge must be coming from somewhere. When you finally accept that you're getting guidance from somewhere, and then accept that this guidance is from spirit, it's truly a wonderful feeling. The word I'd use here to aid understanding is 'euphoric'. One crucial point to remember is that the finite (us) can't totally understand the infinite (spirit). We can only do our best to understand what spirit is trying to tell us. The subtleness of spirit's language is so gentle; that's why so many people struggle to hear it. You'll also become aware of a deep feeling of love within you, which is the love that spirit wants to share with you. However, you might not immediately understand what's being said to you, but with time and patience, if you want spiritual guidance, you'll receive it in a way that you'll understand. Dreams are one way that spirit will try to communicate with you, but there are many others.

No matter how good or bad a person you think you are, spirit will help you understand what's right and wrong, and you'll be given a chance to right any wrongs in this life, without having to wait until the next life.

Spirit wants everyone to realise they're in control of their own destiny, and it wants to hold you by the hand and guide you to a more fulfilling life, which will lead you closer to God.

Many writers throughout history are now coming forward, via mediums, to tell the world they were spiritually inspired in their work, but they were scared to tell people in their lifetime. One such author is Sir Arthur Conan Doyle. Times are different now. We have freedom of speech, and we can all tell the world what we believe without fear of reprisal. Spirit has given me the strength to stand up for what I believe in. I did, of course, realise I'd be taking a significant risk of being mocked and misunderstood in writing about my experiences, as the world as it stands is very science based, but I knew that I had to take a chance, because if I didn't, it would make me unhappy!

At the beginning of my journey, I too was scared to tell people what I believed. Spirit came to me one night 12 years ago and gave me the confidence to stand up for what I believe and to live the life I was meant to live, not the life I'd lived for other people. Spirit also made it clear to me that it wanted me to understand my journey so I could help other people with theirs.

Every word I've written in this book is spirit inspired and whispered to me from the spirit world – even the title of this book – which spirit made me aware of even before my first book had been published. It's clear to me that spirit is so anxious to spread its love, and I'm anxious to interpret this love in words that everyone around the world will understand, whether they're mediumistic or not. Unbelievably, we're all mediums; it's just that we may not have learnt how to hear spirit yet as it's outside the normal five senses everyone has, which can be scary for anyone. Everyone will eventually realise the importance of words, the importance of the brotherhood of man, and that we're all created from the same spirit. As soon as everyone understands spirit's message, they'll start to understand each other, even when they speak in different tongues.

My spirit messages aren't in any order. They were relayed to me for a purpose, and it's for spirit to know why they're in the given order – I'm merely a vessel who allows myself to be used as a channel.

I don't always know the purpose of the message or whom these messages were intended for, but this is normal for a medium – or so I'm told by the experienced ones amongst us. Mediums are the key-holders who provide each of us with the key to our own door, but they can't guide each of us through our door, as we all need to go through our door on our own so we understand our own journey.

When I have an urge to relay spirit messages, I'm compelled to let spirit work through me, and I often rush to my keyboard to bash out what spirit is telling me. Some fellow spiritual friends tell me I should take more control of when I allow spirit to come through with messages, but I disagree. I feel thrilled and privileged to serve spirit and to serve God, and I consider it an honour for spirit to use me as a tool to help people interpret the word of God.

I aim to fill this book with words of encouragement to help people understand the threads of life and not to fear transitioning from human form to spirit form. Even though I never know to whom my messages are directed, I believe and trust they'll mean many things to different people, so just because I've sometimes included my own interpretation of each message, the message might mean something else to other people. I suggest you use your instincts and life experience to consider your own interpretation.

Even if I only reach one person in the world with my spirit messages, I'll die a happy lady!

God bless and walk tall.
Wendy

CHAPTER 1

In memory of my dad

Before my late father passed to spirit, I was told by spirit that it would be my duty to stand up before my family and talk about my father's life. Subsequently, spirit encouraged me to write the following words. This was one of the first occasions when I started to believe I was receiving messages. It was certainly my first experience of losing a loved one. Even my own mother, after hearing me at this funeral service, said I always know what to say! This was the nicest thing she ever said to me! I never told her that I was channelling spirit as she would not have believed me!

Although it was written for my father, I'm certain some of the words within will relate to many fathers around the world.

> *Isn't it the truth that you can live with someone for a lifetime, but it's only when they aren't with you any more that you realise their value?*
>
> *That's the mark of someone who's special.*
>
> *That's the mark of someone who deserves to be in the light and deserves to be with God.*
>
> *To be remembered as someone who was always there to*

listen; to be remembered as someone who was always there to care; and to be remembered as someone who gave their time and dedication to others without ever asking for anything in return: this is how I remember my dad.

He was so special that no one realised his worth until they were aware he was no longer around.

I always remember that if he ever got a phone call from a member of his family who desperately needed his help, he never thought for a second about his own needs. He'd jump into his car and race to that person to give them aid, and he never wanted anything in return. That's how special my dad was, and he'll remain forever in our hearts and minds.

He was a devoted husband and father, and he told me on numerous occasions that he didn't want to leave his family, particularly towards the end of this life.

But dear Father, it's now your time to put aside your worldly shackles and rest forever more in the hands of God. Only your family knew of your suffering towards the end of your life, but despite this, you were always there when we needed you – sometimes pushing aside your own pain to aid others. None of us got a chance to say goodbye; everything happened so quickly. You drifted off to sleep and never regained consciousness.

Dear Father, you may have passed to the spirit world, but you'll forever be in our hearts and minds, and so you will be forever with us – just as you wanted!

Rest in peace, Dad, until we meet each other on the other side...

CHAPTER 2

In memory of my mother

Three years after the death of my dear departed father, I also lost my mother, and in the same way spirit made me aware to prepare for my father's death, it also prepared me for my mother's passing by helping me with the words to celebrate her life.

The first memory of my mother is how hard she worked to keep a lovely home for my sister and me. We never went without anything. In her words: she'd rather feed us and do without herself.

People she met might have viewed her as a trifle pessimistic. The truth is that she was a realist and always tried to help people understand the situation they were in.

It's obvious that, from an early age, she'd learnt the meaning of family and the importance of respecting money. Consequently, her memories stayed with her for a lifetime, and she endeavoured to pass those values on to her family.

In her later years towards the end of her life, much to her surprise, she was blessed with a grandson, Alexander, whom she adored, and it made me incredibly happy to see how much

3

she loved him. In the past, she'd told me that she'd lost a boy herself, her firstborn, and she wondered whether my son was in fact her firstborn reincarnated. Spirit had told me that her firstborn's name was Stephen. [Spirit gave me that specific spelling of his name.]

I always knew my mother was incredibly careful and never did anything in haste. Much to my surprise, I found a parking ticket on which she'd written my son's birth date and weight. She'd kept this in a drawer in her bedroom for 21 years, which I discovered shortly after my mother's passing.

She always took hundreds of photographs of her one and only grandson; I'm going to put them together in an album, which I know would make her happy.

The people who knew my mother loved her. She had an air about her that would put at ease anyone who was in trouble. I don't doubt for a moment she'll be helping people in heaven now, and they're lucky to have her.

Despite the valiant efforts of Good Hope Hospital, which tried to revive her both at home and in the hospital, she died very suddenly, and they were unable to save her. The fact that she didn't suffer is the only consolation her family can take from her sudden death.

I'm glad you're now at peace, Mom. We're all going to miss you!

Until we meet again...

CHAPTER 3

Treasure special moments

The aim of this passage is to help people treasure special moments. The story behind this passage is that I wrote it as a blog in 2015, but I never rediscovered it until 2022. Spirit wanted me to see how I'd grown, to provide me with encouragement to continue with my work, and to provide me with the passage I thought I'd lost.

At the time of finishing *Spirit Writer* in 2022, I started to feel that spirit was guiding me again to continue with my second book. At this time, spirit reminded me of a passage that I'd written when I was at the beginning of my journey, whilst I was attending a Pilgrim's Progress Workshop at Erdington Christian Spiritualist Church. During this class, the teacher told us to write a spirit-inspired message. I can remember placing this spirit message inside a folder, and I never thought about it again. I told spirit in my mind that I'd lost it as I'd thrown my old folder away, and I never thought any more about it until one evening in 2022 when I was considering how to market my first book.

I now know it's normal for me to be directed to things, and I've learnt to let my fingers work of their own accord to show me the way. This was amazing, as anyone who has any experience of Google will realise how hard it is to find things on the internet that you've lost. On reading the blog, I was shocked to find that it contained the message that I'd asked spirit to help me find. This is just one example of how spirit helps me with tasks I feel are impossible.

In this passage, spirit was telling me to treasure special moments. It told me this on the evening of our dear departed Queen Elizabeth II's funeral. This passage was lost between 2015 and 2022, and I was reminded of the same to remember this special moment.

A bird flies high up into the sky, soaring and swooping, surveying the world below. Through his eyes, we now look up high into the clouds.

On the ground below, small animals frolic in the fields.

Water is babbling in the brook, for forever and a day.

Children can be heard playing in the field, gurgling and squeaking. They try to catch butterflies, swooping their net.

The moment is frozen in time, for they only know that moment. They can't see into the future, and they have little knowledge of the past. They'll remember that moment in time one day, when everything was so simple, so clear and so focused.

Their love and laughter can be heard for miles by the spirits above. They smile, and their hearts fill with joy when they see the children playing.

Freeze that moment in time forever and a day, so they may remember this moment for always.

CHAPTER 4

Spirit wants to speak to you

The aim of this passage is to help people who are mourning their loved one who believe they'll never hear their voice again. Unknown to them, spirit is still around, and it will endeavour to help that person hear their loved one again!

I'm trying to speak to you. I'm trying to share my love. I'm trying to share my memories.

You think you can't hear me, but you can!

My words won't be words like you're used to. They'll be like the sounds of a rustling tree, so listen carefully as spirit messages enter and leave your mind quickly, so you must be alert.

You think I'm far away, but I'm closer than you think. I am but a thought away whenever you need my support.

You wish you'd said certain words to me before I passed. Don't worry, I heard you speak those words to me in your thoughts.

I now feel what you felt, and I see what you've seen and what you see now.

I'm here when you need me and hear what you say to me.
I'll hold your hand when you need me and stroke your
face to reassure you I'm around.
Always remember that you'll never be alone again!

CHAPTER 5

What spiritualism means to me

The aim of this passage is to describe how much spiritualism means to me, which I hope will help people consider whether it is for them.

[Spiritualism is now recognised as a religion. Spiritualists believe that the spirit of a dead person can communicate with the living through a medium; for more details, see the website given in the reference (Spiritualists' National Union (n.d)].

I used to follow the crowd.

I used to listen to what the world said to me.

I used to believe what I was told to believe.

I used to cry when the world told me to cry and laugh when the world told me to laugh.

Minutes turned into hours, hours turned into days, days turned into nights, and nights turned into years, with my mind searching for answers to endless questions.

Years passed. I couldn't understand why there was so much I didn't understand and why I was constantly seeking new directions.

Then, one day, or I should say one night, spirit came into my life.

One night, one dream, one moment, and my life was changed forever.

From then on, I no longer listened to the person next to me. I no longer listened to the world. I listened to my inner self, my spirit, and no one can take that away from me – even if they don't believe me.

My inner soul. My inner spirit. I now feel the oneness with spirit, and I know I'll never feel alone again.

I've now accepted that I'm spirit, and that spirit has been with me my whole life, but I didn't take the time to listen. I'm happy that spirit is now in my life, which has helped me love myself again!

I'm now no longer unhappy. I'm now no longer seeking answers, as the answers are whispered to me. I always had the answers, but I just didn't believe that I was worthy. I now know that I am! You too are worthy!

Now that I accept that I'm one with spirit, and I take the time to listen, the love is always there waiting for me.

I'm now complete.

I am spirit.

CHAPTER 6

The personal responsibility of words

T he aim of this passage is to remind people of the personal responsibility they have to help their children understand and respect the meaning and importance of words.

I'm sure that, at some point, we've all said the wrong words to someone we love or we've said the right words and seen a tremendous turnaround, not only in your life but in the lives of everyone to whom you're connected. Think about all the words you've said and the words you've received during your lifetime, and consider the impact they've had on your life and other's lives. It takes only a second to say a wrong word and a lifetime to take it back.

I can remember a teacher told me when I was a child at school, 'You are never going to be...' This is the worst thing a child can hear at school, especially from an authority figure such as a teacher. This tells us that people in authority should be more mindful of their words than ever.

Some people don't realise the true power of words.

They can start a war or stop a war.

They can express love or hate.

They can build bridges or destroy them.

They can be used to pray to your God or to blame God for your own misgivings.

They can write a story, or they can destroy a soul.

Music can be a beautiful sound. Music can be a horrid sound. The first will leave you with a feeling of euphoria. The second will leave you with a headache.

When handing out words, think about what they'll portray to those who receive them.

A baby's first words and every word this child speaks thereafter will impact the world in ways you can't comprehend; therefore, you must teach them to appreciate the true power of words. Once your child has control over their words, they'll be able to conquer anything that may happen in their short lives. So, when teaching your child their first words, I'd suggest you think about how they might use these words in the future. This level of personal responsibility is huge, but it's so important for a child to understand the impact their words can have.

They can portray love or they can portray hate; which words would you like to receive? The first may make you smile. The second may leave you bitter.

They can make or break a court case: one wrong word could cost you your freedom, with you then spending a lifetime in jail. This teaches us the importance of employing a good solicitor, who can use the right words to fight for your freedom!

I hope my words leave you with food for thought.

CHAPTER 7

The sea of life

The aim of this passage is to compare the troubles and turmoil of life to the ebb and flow of the waves at sea, to help people understand the overall picture of one's life journey.

The journey of life is like a tiny boat on the ocean waves.

Some days, the water is like a mill pond, and you can glance at the water to see your own reflection.

At other times, the water is a bit choppy and cloudy, and you must use your oars to guide your tiny boat.

Other times, the water can be as ferocious as a cat, lapping against the sides of your boat, and you wonder when the sea will ever be calm again.

Remember that challenging times may lie ahead, but these times will make you stronger – stronger to fight the unknown.

Like the sea, the trials of your life might seem vast, but if people stand together, it will feel like the trickle of a stream. This standing together focuses on the 'brotherhood of man' principle, which is the second principle of spiritualism.

[The Seven Principles form the basis of the Spiritualists' National Union's spiritualism, and they help spiritualists to navigate and combine their spiritual and human journeys. The Seven Principles provide a positive moral and ethical framework upon which people can base their lives. They were given to us through the mediumship of Emma Hardinge Britten, and they are adopted by those who choose spiritualism as their religion. They are as follows

1 The fatherhood of God

2 The brotherhood of man

3 The communion of spirits and the ministry of angels.

4 The continuous existence of the human soul

5 Personal responsibility

6 Compensation and retribution hereafter for all the good and evil deeds done on earth

7 External progress is open to every human soul

(Spiritualists' National Union (n.d) (See the website given in the reference for more details.)]

CHAPTER 8

Loneliness

The aim of this passage is to help us understand that, at this moment in time, everyone gives different meanings to words, maybe because of their background or maybe because of the language they speak. Spirit is telling us here that it can see a time in the future when mankind will all speak the same language and will all understand each other, no matter what background or country they come from.

When I spoke this message, it was taped by a German lady who told me she felt comfort from it as she'd been feeling lonely. You'll notice I said 'spoke' when I usually write my messages.

Many people have many different thoughts.

Many people only listen to their own thoughts; understanding them isn't always easy.

When there's understanding, there's happiness and no sadness.

We should realise we're not alone.

Spirit sends love to us and words that are needed.

When we're all aware, people will understand.

The knowledge comes down to everyone who's ready to receive it. Some people may question spirit intelligence, but the knowledge only comes to those that are ready for it.

Ask, and the true meaning of love will come to us, and then everyone will be together as one.

We'll be one voice, with no separation of language.

We'll understand each other.

When people work together and stand together, they won't stand apart, and everyone will share the love.

Stop and listen. Stop and share!

CHAPTER 9

Reflection in the water

The aim of this passage is to help people see what others see, and spirit is suggesting looking into a pool of water and glancing at your own reflection. Spirit is telling us that, one day, we'll see what others see. Although this passage is short, it's very poignant!

Glance into the water; what do you see?

Glance into the water; what do other people see?

A time will come when you realise it will no longer matter what you see; you'll only care what other people see. You'll look into the water and see your brother, not yourself. When that time comes, you'll finally realise that we're all the same. You'll no longer wish to be better than your brother, because we'll all have the same understanding of what's important.

That time can't come about until we start to care for one another in the way in which we wish other people would care for us. [This is the second principle, the brotherhood of man.]

When this understanding comes about, there will no

longer be any fear. There will no longer be any hate. There will only be love.

You don't have to wait until you return to spirit before you seek forgiveness and guidance; you can make changes now. [This is the sixth principle: compensation and retribution hereafter for all the good and evil deeds done on earth.]

Now is the time, and now is the moment.

CHAPTER 10

Burn your candle brightly

The aim of this passage is to help people not to be scared to stand up for what they believe, and to burn their candle brightly.

It was my grandmother who first compared me to a candle that attracts people to its light. She told me, during my spirit dream 12 years ago, that she couldn't look at me when I was a child because my light was so bright. She said that I must have thought she didn't care for me, but this wasn't the case; it was just that my light was too bright for her to gaze upon for too long. I never forgot this message, and throughout my life, other mediums have relayed the same message to me, so I realised this message must be true.

The last time I heard someone refer to my light was at a Sunday service at my local church, when a well-known medium who sees auras (Jacqui Rogers) was instantly drawn to me. She told me that my light was filling the church and I must be a soldier of God. This took me by surprise, as before, only my grandmother had outright referred to 'my light'. Immediately, I knew that spirit was reminding me of my task upon the earth and my duty to God!

This is also a short passage, but I believe it's very meaningful.

> *Burn your candle brightly when you want others to see who you are.*
>
> *Your light will attract people to you who want to bask in the blaze of your flame.*
>
> *When this happens, you'll no longer be worried about your own problems; you'll be more concerned about other people's problems, and this will help you forget about your own problems.*

The more I think about this passage, the more I realise spirit is reminding me that the time has come for me to forget about my own problems and to start to care about other people's problems.

CHAPTER 11

Accepting death as part of life

The aim of this passage is to make people aware of what it's like to be on your deathbed and what kind of thoughts might be going through your mind as you lie quietly waiting for death to claim you. Some might consider this to be morbid, but spirit is trying to help us understand that we won't be alone at this time; we are just transitioning from the physical state to the spiritual state from whence we came. It's my belief that spirit is constantly reminding us that we need not fear death!

You lie in your bed waiting for death to claim you.

You lie in your bed, scared of the unknown.

People visit you from your past. They come to tell you what you mean to them. They come to tell you your true worth. These are the spirits of your loved ones who are coming to hold your hand on your final journey.

You're looking through a haze, and you're no longer certain what everything means. Trust what you hear. Trust what you see.

Feel the love that's being brought to you.

Hold your loved ones' hands and let them guide you to the light. Don't be scared. Just let yourself drift into the sea of love and light!

CHAPTER 12

Fear of the unknown

The aim of this passage is to help people not to be scared of the unknown.

Fear can be very destructive and hold us back from the journey that was meant for us. I now know this is what held me back for much of my life, but on a positive note, if I hadn't felt fear, I wouldn't have felt the glory that was bestowed upon me later in life. Everything is for a purpose!

People want to believe there's more to this life, but many fear the unknown, so they're sometimes scared to look for it. There's only one way to stop fearing the unknown, and that's through knowledge – knowledge not just from people on the earthly plane who've had spiritual experiences, but also from learning to listen to your inner messages from your spirit guides, and from learning to trust your intuition.

A lack of knowledge breeds fear, which can be disruptive to your life and make you believe things that aren't true. You need to find out the truth to help you relieve yourself of this fear.

I too feared the unknown at the beginning of my journey, and that's why I started to make a mental note of strange events in my life, so I could try to understand what was going on. I knew I was taking a chance that no one would believe me, but I had to take that chance, as spirit was trying to help me stand up for what I believed in so I could help others. I knew I was experiencing strange occurrences, and I became aware that I was remembering key events in my life, but I didn't know why at the time. As soon as I overcome my fear, with spirit guidance, I became strong.

It has taken me a lifetime to come to terms with the fact that I was experiencing spirit phenomena, so I decided to write everything down in my first book, *Spirit Writer*, in the hope that it might help even one person who has experienced similar phenomena. Spirit will try to help us in many ways; we just need to find the time to listen. I now know I took the wrong turns in life because I didn't make the time to listen.

In the beginning, I saw what I thought were visions, which I now know to be spirit, but I'm hearing spirit more clearly now. Spirit knows that I'm now listening to it, and the more that I listen, the more it's using my abilities to write my many messages. Often, spirit will feature in our dreams, and if it believes you're listening to it, it will also try to communicate with you in the daytime.

I invite you to come to terms with what you're afraid of in your life and to take this fear by the horns!

CHAPTER 13

Memories and the loss of the Queen

The aim of this passage is to help people realise the importance of memories.

My granddad (in spirit) has just reminded me of my own special memories of when he gave me my first home-grown tomato to taste and when he built me my first doll's house. These are a few of my special memories, so let's consider why some events become memories for us and why other moments are forgotten.

What defines a memory? What defines a special moment? Why do we remember some things and not others?

Some might say we could be remembering things from a previous life; this may be true. Our likes and dislikes appear at an early age, so again, this may be why. We certainly like things or dislike things for a reason. Or could it be the way these occurrences are presented to us that determine whether they become good or bad memories.

Whatever the reason we remember our memories, it's certain they'll impact our future lives, be it for good or bad reasons. We might not understand those reasons at the time, but it's likely that we'll be reminded of them in our future to help us understand that things happen for a reason.

Memories can also be a connection, or a bond, between loved ones – just like when my grandfather let me taste my first tomato. My grandfather is making me remember this bond at this time so he can remind me about the importance of memories and deep bonds that we should make with our fellow man. I realise now that my grandfather is linking this memory theme to the memory of the loss of Queen Elizabeth II and reminding me to remember this moment, as it's a special moment and one I'll only experience once in my lifetime!

CHAPTER 14

What's in a name?

The aim of this passage is to help people understand the importance of using a correct name tag to describe themselves to others so they don't lead others to believe something they're not.

Do you find that some people these days are giving themselves a name tag that often doesn't truly represent who or what they are? I'm inspired this evening to talk about being careful regarding listening to the wrong people when seeking spiritual guidance. You must listen to many people before you find the right person to help you understand your journey. I hope you gain something from this passage.

You must discover the right door to go through to change your life. Sometimes, you must go through quite a few doors before you find your ultimate door, which will lead you to your pathway, but don't let this dishearten you, because you'll eventually appreciate the end goal even more when you've experienced the journey!

Have you noticed how people are hung up on calling themselves a certain name, hoping that people will believe they have certain skills that are attached to this name. In the end, it doesn't matter what we call ourselves so long as our words and actions are said and done in good faith, and we don't deceive people into believing something that isn't true.

People have the right to believe or not believe what you say, as we all have free will, so there's nothing wrong with this, but there are those who won't even consider what you say and poke fun without having true understanding.

You can give someone the key to their door, but you can't make them go through their door. If people don't believe what you say, aren't prepared to do research themselves to deepen their knowledge, and are being negative, then it's difficult to help that person find their way. Can you imagine how frustrating it must be for a spirit guide who's wanting to help someone, but they can't even begin to help until that person acknowledges them and isn't scared. That's how patient spirit is. Sometimes, spirit guides must wait a lifetime, but they'll never give in. They're persistent and they'll keep trying to help you understand in many ways. Remember spirit has no perception of time!

If you open your heart and mind to the spiritual side of life, you'll receive messages. These messages might come in the form of dreams or they might be in the form of sending someone to help us understand a situation. I know this to be true, as that's what happened to me on my journey: spirit sent many people my way to help me believe in the existence of spirit and to believe in my spiritual gifts so I could help people who were drawn to my light.

At this moment in time, many people are claiming they have spiritual abilities, and they call themselves many names, and each person who visits them is expecting a different thing from their visit. However, what they expect often comes from their perception of what has been said and experienced throughout their life – the contents of which might be right *and might be wrong. This is the reason people are dissatisfied with spiritual guidance given by people who claim they are this or that. They're trying to understand situations without having enough knowledge to make their own decisions.*

I believe spiritual guidance should be focused on spiritual philosophy, for only when you understand this will you understand and eventually believe in your pathway. The essence of spiritualism is philosophy, and only by understanding this will you understand the words of God.

Remember, finding your pathway starts with trying to find your key, and once you've found your key, you must then find your door to use that key in. Don't forget, it's you who must go through that door on your own, which can often be a long path.

Following a spiritual path is not easy, but I'm sure of one thing: once you've found your door, you'll find happiness and love that you've never experienced before!

Don't fear trying a few door handles until you find the door that's meant for you!

CHAPTER 15

The joy of music

The aim of this passage is to help people appreciate the joy of music.

Throughout the whole of my life, I've loved music; I've used it as an escape from the world around me – escape from things I didn't understand. I now know that the sounds I was trying to block out at an early age were the sounds of my spirit guides, who didn't wish me harm; they came to show me the way!

Due to my lifelong love of music, I feel it only fitting that I pay homage to the many people of our time who either sing or play an instrument, and in doing so, they bring so much joy to others, helping people to forget their troubles and join with their brothers and sisters in a moment of peace and serenity.

Oh how sweet the sound of a melody to herald a moment in time!

Forget about your troubles and let your mind dance to the sounds of the angels. Let your foot tap to the rhythm and let your body sway from side to side.

Don't worry if you can't dance. Don't worry if you can't

sing. No one will be watching you, except your God. No one will be listening to you singing, except your God.

Sing and dance like your life depends on it. Bob and weave. Tip and tap your feet. Float around the dancefloor and let your heart sing with joy.

Forget who you are for a moment. Pretend you're a king. Pretend you're a princess.

Swing and sway, moving your partner this way and that. You're whoever you want to be when you let your favourite music float around your mind like the sea ebbs and flows on the seashore.

Bow your head in reverence to the masters of the world of music because they deserve respect for connecting people in many special ways, helping people forget their physical self for a moment and reminding them they are spirit without them even realising it.

CHAPTER 16

Time

The aim of this passage is to help people appreciate and value *time*.

When do we get an awareness of time? This is a good starting point because it's only when we get that awareness of it that we become anxious about the passage of time and are concerned we won't have enough time to do this or that.

For sure, the older we get, the more anxious we become about time running out; we start to regret what we haven't done with our lives, believing we'll never get a second chance to put things right.

It certainly isn't possible to go back in time, but it is possible to embrace the here and now, and you don't have to wait until the afterlife before you decide that you want to put right wrongs of the past and change your life for the good. In fact, by taking control of your life now, you're making an early start on transforming your life when you return to your spiritual existence. [This is the sixth principle: compensation and retribution hereafter for all the good and evil deeds done on earth]

No matter whether we're good or bad, we all return to spirit in the end, because that's where we came from and that's where we'll return to – remember we're our own judge and jury!

When I was at a crossroads in my life 12 years ago, I wanted to know the reason I was so dissatisfied with my life, despite having fulfilled all the usual earthly desires people have. My life started to change when I started asking questions that, subsequently, I received answers to when I started to listen to and hold love for spirit in my heart. I thought I wasn't aware of spirit from an early age, I now realise that it has always been with me, trying to help me find my way. Of course, at the time, I didn't realise that my many questions were being answered. It was just that I wasn't listening and believing. Now, at the tender age of 57, I realise that it's only when I ask questions that I receive answers.

Remember when I spoke about my concern about losing a lovely spirit message that I wrote in 2015, which I believed I'd never find again? It was only when I had this question in my mind regarding where this passage was that it appeared on my screen shortly thereafter.

Even though I'm now becoming more aware of how spirit is working with me, it wasn't until this moment that I realised my questions were really, truly being answered – all I needed to do was trust!

I've seen and felt many wonderous things as a medium, but I'm still learning to understand how spirit is working with me.

The fact that I'm now writing about time indicates to me that spirit doesn't want us to be frightened of time, but that we are to embrace it to remind us to focus on what we want to achieve in the time we have left on the earthly plane, and there-after when we return to spirit.

> *Part of our earthly existence is about learning; we never stop learning, and making mistakes is part of learning. So if you find you've hit a crossroads, take a breath, take time to decide which direction to go in next, and follow the direction you believe is right for you. You'll find that, by taking stock and asking for guidance, it will give you time to consider your way forwards or your next step.*
>
> *Imagine for a moment that you're walking through a beautiful, wooded area with a trickling stream beneath your feet. Behind you are the stepping stones of the past, and in front of you are the stepping stones of the future. If you've come to a crossroads and wonder whether you should go this way or that, stand for a moment on the stone that's your turning point and look ahead at the obstacles in front of you.*
>
> *But don't forget how far you've come, as it's because of your past that you are where you are now, be it right or wrong. Only you will know whether your past was right or wrong. It is for you to consider before you move on. You have personal responsibility for your life, and you should not blame others for your mistakes.*

In my case, I didn't fully appreciate my journey until I came to a pathway later in life, and I realised the reason I was being inspired to remember my life was so I could understand my future.

CHAPTER 17

The wonder of life

The aim of this passage is to help people fully appreciate *the wonder of life* and all it entails.

I stand on the precipice of life, looking down upon the world and gazing high into the sky in one fleeting glance. At this moment in time, I can feel no pain, no sorrow. I stand in awe, admiring how boundless and wonderous the world is. Every crevice of land is teaming with life. Every drop of sea is teaming with life. Every breath of air is teaming with life. Nothing is wasted in nature. Life and death are so intertwined that, sometimes, it's difficult to know when life starts and when it ends; but does the animal kingdom worry? No.

The swoop of the wand of Father God might seem ruthless to mankind, but mankind must remember there's a time to live and a time to die; that's the circle of life. Animals don't worry where the next meal is coming from; they see their babies surrounding them, and they know instantly they must go out into the world and gather food to fill their bellies. The chicks grow into strong birds, and their mother dies, but the chicks don't worry about the death of their mother; they lift their tiny wings and fly high into the sky, just like their mother taught them, and they start the circle of life again.

We can learn a lot from Mother Nature!

CHAPTER 18

Be like a rose

T he aim of this passage is to help people realise how important they are to God. I'm being shown a rose – a beautiful, red rose – and I'm reminded how easy it is to exist as such. It's this simplicity that spirit wants us to think of when we're troubled.

Being a rose is so simple and so beautiful.

Whatever the rose wants, Mother Earth provides.

It doesn't have to think about what to do, and what not to do.

It doesn't have to ask for what it needs.

If it needs rainwater to drink, it's provided by Mother Earth.

If it needs nourishment, it's provided by Mother Earth.

If it needs sunlight, it's provided by Mother Earth.

If it wants to pollinate other roses, it doesn't consider how or why; Mother Earth sends a bee to dart from one rose to another, spreading the beauty of nature throughout the world.

If the rose wants to show its beauty, it simply opens its petals and shows its beauty with pure innocence.

It never asks for anything; it doesn't need to as everything is provided by Mother Earth for the rose to sustain its beauty.

Wouldn't it be nice if we could live our lives as simply as the rose?

Wouldn't it be nice if we had no worries, and everything was taken care of by Mother Earth? It is. It's just that we don't appreciate the beauty of what gifts we have until it's too late.

If everything is provided for the rose without it even asking, why do we doubt that everything will be provided to us, as in our form, we're closer to God than the rose is?

The rose doesn't doubt or question, and yet it flourishes for a moment in time, but what beauty it displays in the little time that remains!

It simply exists. It simply is.

We come from the earth and we return to the earth, just like the rose, and yet we have so many questions and so many doubts despite being provided with gifts that the rose will never have – yet a rose doesn't doubt or cry!

Wouldn't it be fine if we could believe without wanting proof?

Wouldn't it be fine if we could accept the help that's available to us without doubting?

Walk through a rose garden, touch the petals and smell the sweet perfume surrounding you, taking care not to touch the thorns. [That's how spirit is telling us to live our lives: with an air of simplicity like the rose, but to always be aware that we're personally responsible for our actions, which is what spirit means by 'take care not to touch the thorns'.]

Nature surrounds us with beauty every day, yet we don't always appreciate it. Take the time to appreciate the beauty of nature and don't question, just accept – like the rose.

CHAPTER 19

The place of God

T he aim of this passage is to help people understand *the place of God* in the religion of spiritualism. (This is the first principle of spiritualism).

Everything in nature has a place, a start and an end. A time to be born and a time to die. God and the Natural Law play a key role in spiritualism.

From considering the accounts of many mediums of the past, my own experiences and my connection with God, I believe that he doesn't want to be seen as the vengeful God of old, as portrayed by the Church. He wants to empower people to take responsibility for their own actions and to take charge of their own destiny, embracing their fellow men as 'equals no matter what their position'. It's also clear that it's only by being 'of one mind with our brothers' that the world will understand the meaning of God and the Natural Laws of the Universe.

Even before I was aware of my spiritual connection, I always felt an inner connection with God, despite being brought up in a family who didn't believe in the same thing. I never realised at that time that the knowledge being bestowed on me, even from an early age, was from God and my spirit guides.

I used to think I had a vivid imagination as a child, as I had no one around me with spiritual knowledge. It took me most of my life to discover the truth – the truth about love, the truth about life and the truth about family – not just our own family, but the family of our brotherhood of man, whom spirit tells us we should try to connect with to enable us to become closer to our Father God.

> *There's no need to fear God. There's no need to fear birth. There's no need to fear death. There's no need to fear anything – that's spirit's message. At all times, we're with our loved ones, who are surrounding us with their love and guidance should we ever need it; and when it becomes time for our transition to return to our spiritual existence, they'll be there waiting for us in the light, holding out their arms to take us on the next stage of our spiritual journey.*

CHAPTER 20

World of dreams

The aim of this passage is to portray how important the world of dreams has been in helping me understand spirit messages.

As a child, I couldn't wait until bedtime when I could drift in the land of make-believe. Many a time I didn't know what was real and what was a dream state. To this day, I'm still an avid dreamer, and since I've learnt that spirit comes to us in our dreams, I appreciate this special time even more. As dreams are so important, both to me and spirit, I felt it important to write a few words on the world of dreams.

The world of dreams is a world of make-believe. It's a time in which your mind can drift and your body can rest. It's a time when you can forget who you are and imagine who you'd like to be. It's a time when you can become closer to your loved ones. It's a time when you become closer to your God. In your dreams, you lose your inhibitions and you let go, like a puff of smoke. Your spiritual body is no longer held back by your physical body, so it can be spirit once more.

Without even realising it, our bodies constantly yearn to

return to spirit; spirit describes returning to the spirit world as being just like when you take off your coat. We aren't scared of taking off our attire, and so we mustn't fear being released from our physical body and returning to our spiritual body. Spirit tells us the importance of learning to let go of the past so we can be free to live our future. Let go of the past. Let go of our physical self. Only when we learn how to do this will we hold hands with our loved ones again and, eventually, hold the hands of our God.

CHAPTER 21

The importance of healing

T he aim of this passage is to help people understand
the importance of healing in the world.
During my mediumistic training, I've had
moments when I believed I was struggling to hear spirit clearly.
I couldn't understand how I was struggling to give messages in
class, often just standing silently, my fellow classmates
wondering why, and when I returned home to my sanctuary,
my home, I'd have conversations with spirit.

I always remembered that several mediums had told me
the importance of letting go of the past to move forwards, and
only now do I realise I was being given good advice. After this
guidance, I felt the urge once more to be available to talk to
spirit – not just to listen, but to talk.

I now realise how important healing is for me – not just to
help others, which I've always wanted to do, but to heal
myself! By healing myself – by which I mean releasing the past
from my mind – each time I connect to spirit now, I can hear
it clearer, and I believe this is the importance of this book
to me.

I thought my first book was an important part of my

healing process, but I now realise that this book is an even greater part of my healing journey, as through it, I am helping people understand the part that God plays in everyone's life.

Since my healing practicals, which have been part of my healing course, I've noticed my connection to spirit has increased tremendously. I've been aware of spirit for a long time, but I've sometimes had problems hearing everything spirit told me.

I was always aware of spirit's presence, but I sometimes found it difficult to hear its messages and I now realise the reason why was that I needed to heal. I recognise now that the way spirit likes to work with me is like a mother would hold a baby – this is the only way I can describe it.

Over the last 12 years, many mediums have told me healing is important to me, but I've had to find out for myself just how important. In the beginning, I didn't know whether healing was for me, but since completing my healing training I recognise that it is part of me – part of my spiritual make-up.

Once again, spirit has shown me the way to use my spirit writing to help me listen to its words. I can't believe how clearly I can now hear spirit. Sometimes, I have a tear running down my face as I feel the beauty and the divinity of spirit when it relays messages to me!

Spirit has shown me here how beautiful healing is to the world, and we must hold it gently within our hands and gaze at it like it's an iridescent pearl.

CHAPTER 22

Previous lives

T he aim of this passage is to help people understand that we all have a purpose in life, and it's part of our journey to understand that purpose.

When you think of your present life and what you consider has gone right and what has gone wrong, don't be too harsh on yourself. When we make the transition from spirit to physical, we're given choices to achieve certain goals.

For years, I had a heavy heart because I was thinking I'd made a mess of my life, and that's why, 12 years ago, I said many a prayer asking for guidance on how best to conduct the rest of my life. It's only now, midway into my healing teachings and after my dear grandma whispered in my ear again, do I realise that everything I've gone through and the distance I've travelled, whether painful or joyful, was planned for me before I even came back to exist as 'Wendy'. Spirit wanted me to understand life in order that I could help other people on their journey, and it was only when I had a lifetime's worth of experiences that I realised everything was meant to be.

I'm not saying there won't be occasions when you might go down the wrong road due to earthly influences, but I think it's safe to say that – no matter how painful this might be to hear, so please forgive me – most of your journey was more than likely planned, and it was your ultimate goal to understand something you didn't understand from a previous life. So dear heart, don't feel too bitter of heart when wondering whether the mistakes in your life were all due to yourself. Be joyful, as I genuinely believe that, if you're reading my words, it's because you were meant to be reading my words. Please don't think I'm being overzealous with this remark. I was meant to write. I am a spirit writer. I was meant to teach. I was meant to hold your hand to help you realise you've come a long way if you're reading my words.

If you realise where you've gone wrong, you should have a good idea which road to go down next. Forgive me if my words sound hard to grasp. Feel my words within your heart and remember that you can only go forwards – you can't go back.

Move forwards with love and don't look back.

Believe in your heart that you're now on the right road!

CHAPTER 23

Do animals have souls?

The aim of this passage is to help mankind understand the place that animals have within the world.

Why do we foolishly think we're the only presence on the earth that has a soul? We boast about our intelligence and then demonstrate our lack of compassion for others, which suggests there's something missing in our spiritual make-up.

I liken the beauty and simplicity of animals to a newborn human baby who doesn't understand what they're feeling, what they're seeing, what they're hearing, and their need for food and drink. Despite all this lack of knowledge, they instinctively demonstrate they know what's right and wrong, and they hold their little arms open with unconditional love for their parents, just like our loved ones open their arms for us, welcoming us back into the light!

Spirit suggests we'll need to return to this inner knowing if we're to truly prepare for our return to our spiritual existence, so as to show to the great divine that we've learnt compassion for our fellow man during our earthly existence.

Consider how dogs can be trained to sniff out substances, to catch criminals, to provide company to old people, or to serve people with disabilities (such as those who are blind), helping them discover a new life and keep them free from harm. I'd challenge anyone who doubts that these animals have love in their hearts and that they don't each have a soul.

They might not be able to talk, but they demonstrate daily that they want to please their owner and they're willing to serve and devote their life to their owner. They show their unconditional love in ways that many humans couldn't possibly comprehend, never asking for anything in return, and making us warm and fuzzy inside.

Whatever happens in the earthly world, animals seek to show us the way without asking for anything in return.

CHAPTER 24

Through the eyes of a wolf

T he aim of this passage is for mankind to consider
what it's like to be a wolf. This passage demonstrates
once more the unconditional love that spirit has for
us and suggests picturing yourself as a wolf cub to understand
what's important to them. It's another example from nature
of the 'brotherhood of man' principle [the second principle].

*My first memory: huddled close to my mother's teat, her soft
skin and fur enveloping me. I chomp away, filling my mouth
full of her life-preserving milk, the excess dribbling around
my gaping jaws, with my eyes tightly shut as I savour the taste.
I gulp for air in between filling my mouth with sweet nectar –
the nectar of the gods.*

My siblings surround me, fighting for the best position.

*I notice that I feel stronger and stronger as the moon
above rises and falls.*

*I notice that sounds around me are becoming more
distinct and new smells are filling my nostrils, sending visions
into my mind that I'm beginning to understand.*

Dominance prevails amongst my kind, the weaker

following the stronger, but that doesn't mean we don't care for one another. As we become stronger, we play-fight amongst ourselves, demonstrating to each other who'll be the next leader. In our world, we must prove we're worthy to be the leader, but our dominance has a purpose and is not cruel like it is in the world of men.

As our legs grow long, as our ears prick up, as our snouts grow and as our fangs get more pronounced, our appetite grow for more sustaining meat to fill our bellies, making sure no one goes hungry.

To the outside world, we must appear to be ferocious, scrabbling for our next meal, but only we know how gentle we are, guiding and nurturing our fellow pack members, with the stronger protecting the weaker. (This is the closeness that spirit wishes us to have with our fellow man and refers to the second principle: the brotherhood of man.)

We soon learn the importance of the moon, and how we stay connected with our pack by sending mesmerising howls into the night sky. Our howls not only help each member of the pack to be aware of each other's location but also serve to remind each other that we're all as one! To us, that sound is important because it makes us feel stronger when we're together as one.

CHAPTER 25

The Tree of Life

T he aim of this passage is to help people understand the circle of life.

When a seed was placed in my mind a number of years ago about the Tree of Life, its connections with Christianity and its even deeper roots with the Kabbalah, I became increasingly fascinated with what the Tree of Life represents. I knew it was portraying something special, but it would take me many years before I fully understood what it signifies. For this reason, I'll connect with spirit here to help us get a deeper understanding of it.

The Tree of Life represents all aspects of life and has been referred to from the beginning of time.

Its branches. Its roots. Its fruit.

It's both good and evil at the same time. Just as man is good and evil at the same time.

It reaches high with its branches, and it touches God.

It reaches low with its roots, seeking out man-made desires.

It bears fruit in the summer sun, which represents

mankind's need to reach high up into the sky for the fruit of the Lord. The tree can only bear fruit if it reaches up high, so we too can only taste the fruit if we reach high into the sky, aiming for the sun, the stars and the moon.

The bark surrounding the tree grows thicker and stronger, so we must do the same.

Our path will never be an easy one, but how sweet the fruit will be if we nurture our seed – the seed that was planted by our Lord – and it's for us to nurture that seed so we too can become trees. (This relates to the personal responsibility principle.)

In the midnight sky, the moon and the stars dance, filling the dark void. The light will always prevail and swallow up the darkness, but a tree needs to be nurtured for it to blossom, and it can only be nurtured by the light of the Lord, without which it will wither and die.

So, we too will wither and die if we don't stand firm and strong, waving our arms in the air like a tree waves its branches in the cool breeze.

CHAPTER 26

The connection between the two worlds

T he aim of this passage is to help people understand the connection between the spirit world and the physical world. Spirit inspired me with this title, showing me two planets displayed on my computer screen so I'd understand the close connection between the spirit world and the physical world.

Spirit communication is very visual for me, and it often shows me images that it knows I'll understand. It works with me this way, as it knows I have a pictorial brain. It will work with you on whatever level is appropriate, so you'll understand what it's saying to you. Spirit sees no barrier between language and culture; it will communicate to you in a way that you understand. Spirit wants all humanity to develop the same understanding so we recognise that we're all one, and if we hurt our fellow humans, we're hurting ourselves.

Spirit is inspiring me to write about how close the spirit world is to the physical world, without you even realising this. People fear what they think is the unknown. However, what they think is unknown is, in fact, known because it's part of you without you even realising it.

My grandmother reassured me a long time ago that I'd start to become connected to the spirit world. When she told me this, it was only natural that I was initially scared, but she instantly sent love to my heart and mind to demonstrate to me that she'd give her life for mine if she had to. I have no doubt at all now that the love between my grandmother and me is boundless and will be so until the end of time. She has never shown herself to me in spirit form because, in her words, 'I never scared my children when I was alive, and I won't scare them now.'

Those in the physical world are now reaching high and low for answers to understand what's going on around them, so they've got more control over their lives, but they should be looking inside themselves as well.

We're all made up of both a physical and a spiritual presence, and as the physical presence withers like an autumn leaf, your spiritual presence will remain infinite.

I know that spirit won't falter in helping mankind understand how beautiful each person's spirit presence is and that we should nurture this as a farmer nurtures his crop, season after season.

Spirit surrounds the physical world, and the sensitive among us will sense this when they are ready, and not before. It has been like this since the beginning of time, and it will remain like this until the end of our days.

CHAPTER 27

Barnabas – my light and my guide

The aim of this passage is demonstrate the role that my spirit guide, Barnabas, plays in my life.

Many years passed before I knew who my main spirit guide was. He first made me aware that he had religious significance and left it at that. I never pushed him any more as I knew he'd tell me when the time was right. Even before he made me aware of his presence, since I was a young girl I'd always felt I had a deep religious yearning inside me. This concerned my family, and I'd frequently hear them talking about how concerned they were about my obsession with God. The question in their minds was that they weren't religious, so why was I?

As time passed, I accepted what my guide told me. I knew one day he'd tell me his name and his significance in my life when he believed the time was right.

I first became aware of him when I was attending a spiritual awareness class at Erdington Christian Spiritualist Church 12 years ago. One week, we were asked to think about our spirit guides and three guides appeared to me, with the major one calling himself a monk. I also knew that the second one also had a religious significance, and I was aware she was a nun. The third was an Indian who was also deeply spiritual. No wonder I felt religious when I had all these guiding me!

As the years passed, the monk told me his name was Barnabas, but it wasn't until I started mediumistic training years later at Sutton Spiritualist Church that he started to make me more aware of his presence. During this time, a couple of Arthur Findlay College mediums also told me of his existence and of his religious and healing connection. I was told that he admired my positive attitude to life.

When I finally accepted my role was to be a healer, I started to become more aware of how much he wanted to use my healing ability. He never failed to make me aware of his name, telling me constantly he was Barnabas. Eventually, I decided I needed to know more about him, and he told me that he was an early Christian, one of the prominent disciples of Jerusalem.

Oh Barnabas, thank you for connecting with me. Thank you for helping me understand my healing gift! We're stronger together as one.

Barnabas has now made me aware it's time to draw *Pure Spirit* to a close. Now I'm more aware of his presence, I feel stronger for it, and the beauty of his healing energy flows through me like a cool summer breeze!

I'm also being made aware of the Bible quotation I've placed at the beginning of this book to help readers understand that God will stand by you if you stand by him.

The second passage focuses on the title of this book *Pure Spirit*, and explains that pure spirit is inside each of us, it just needs to be awakened!

Bibliography

Spiritual Experience (2022). *The Pure Spirit*. [online] Available at: https://spiritualexperience.eu/pure-spirit [Accessed 22nd October 2022].

Spiritualists' Nationalist Union (n.d.). *Our philosophy & the Seven Principles*. [online] Available at: https://www.snu.org.uk/7-principles. [Accessed 22nd October 2022].

The Bible: King James Version (2022). [online] Available at: https://www.kingjamesbibleonline.org/Luke-Chapter-10/ [Accessed 22nd October 2022].

Acknowledgments

My two special friends:Dorothy Hargreaves, vice principal of
Sutton Coldfield Spiritualist Church; and Lisa Twinks-West.

About the Author

Wendy Sheffield
BA(Hons)

Wendy is a trained legal secretary who has always valued her knowledge and the skills she has worked so hard for. When the time came for her to recognise that the career she had worked so hard for was at an end, she was very sad. To console her, spirit made her aware that she was capable of so much more. Spirit made her aware of her spiritual gifts, which include mediumship, psychic abilities, spirit writing and healing, to name a few, and it sent various people to her to show she should believe in her spiritual guides and to help her realise she had an obligation to help others using her gifts.

One such person that came in her path was an experienced medium who placed two crosses in her hands, whereupon Wendy saw the mother and father of this gentleman and gave a detailed description of them both. He was grateful for the fact that he had never received a connection with his father before.

When Wendy started to use her gifts, she became aware that helping others in turn helped her to forget about the past and to work towards a better future. Her spirit writing became a hobby that helped her cope with the past, and she knew it would help others in the same way.

Wendy now enjoys writing. Her first book is *Spirit Writer: Spiritwriterspeaks*, *Pure Spirit* is her second book, and she is presently working on *My Healing Journey*.

The final message is that this is not the end, it is the beginning...

facebook.com/spiritwriterspeaks

twitter.com/spiritwriteruk

instagram.com/spiritwriterspeaks

Printed in Great Britain
by Amazon

13405843R00047